PROFITABLE STAY-AT-HOME SIDE HUSTLES

The Ultimate Guide to Making Extra Money from Home

Ruth Garner

TABLE OF CONTENTS

INTRODUCTION

The idea of side jobs as a way to get extra money has been increasingly popular in recent years. The concept of work-from-home side business is gaining popularity as more people look for flexible work schedules and methods to supplement their primary source of income. Starting a successful side business from the comfort of your home is now simpler than ever, thanks to the development of technology and online platforms.

Starting a side hustle is an exciting and rewarding way to make extra income while working from the comfort of your own home. With the right mindset and a willingness to work, anyone can launch a successful home-based business. Whether you're looking to supplement your full-time job or eventually transition to self-employment, a home-based side hustle can help you achieve those dreams.

With the right side hustle, you can make money in your spare time without sacrificing your day job or needing to leave the house.

From selling handmade items to taking surveys, there are plenty of ways to make money from the comfort of your home. This book will explore the best stay-at-home side hustles for making extra money and how you can make the most of them.

This book will discuss the steps to get your side hustle, from conducting market research to creating an effective marketing plan. You can launch a profitable side hustle from home with the right strategy and determination.

This book is for you if you want to find a home-based way to make some extra money. "Profitable Stay-At-Home Side Hustles: The Ultimate Guide to Making Extra Money from Home" is a comprehensive book that provides a variety of doable and tested methods for launching and managing prosperous stay-at-home side businesses.

This book contains insightful information and practical advice to get you started, whether you're a student, a stay-at-home parent, or just searching for methods to diversify your income streams.

There are countless ways to make money from home, including online tutoring, freelance writing, Amazon product sales, and running a blog.

This book will give you the information and resources to develop a successful stay-at-home side business using your interests, skills, and talents. So, "Profitable Stay-At-Home Side Hustles" contains all the tools you need to succeed, whether you want to supplement your income or launch a full-time business from home.

So, if you're ready to start your stay-at-home side hustle, read on to discover the most profitable opportunities. With the right approach, you'll be able to make extra money from the comfort of your own home.

CHAPTER ONE

WHAT IS A SIDE HUSTLE

In recent years, pursuing additional income streams through "side hustles" has become a viable option for many people. A supplemental source of revenue that someone pursues in addition to their principal occupation or enterprise is referred to as a "side hustle" Stay-at-home side hustles allow people to generate additional income without leaving the comfort of their own homes, in contrast to those side hustles that need individuals to work away from their houses. In this chapter, we will discuss the advantages of working from home as a side hustle and why such endeavors are gaining popularity.

THE BENEFITS OF STAY-AT-HOME SIDE HUSTLES

The freedom of stay-at-home side hustles is among the significant advantages these types of jobs offer.

Individuals can more efficiently combine their professional and personal lives when they have a stay-at-home side hustle since they may work from the comfort of their own homes on their timetables. This flexibility is especially beneficial for parents who stay at home with their children yet wish to earn additional income while still being available to care for themselves and their families. Working in a relaxed setting, free from the interruptions and pressures of a conventional office environment, is another advantage of working from home in a side hustle or other occupation.

Stay-at-home side hustles give an additional benefit in the form of a low-cost entry point into entrepreneurship.

Most side hustles that can be done from home can be done without a considerable initial investment of either money or resources to get started. For instance, all that is required to engage in freelance writing or graphic design is a computer and access to the internet.

On the other hand, all required to provide pet sitting or house cleaning services are standard supplies and equipment. Because they have such a low barrier to entry, work-from-home side hustles are an appealing choice for anyone interested in generating additional cash.

Stay-at-home side hustles are becoming increasingly popular as people look for ways to supplement their income and make extra money without leaving the comfort of their homes. Many benefits come with taking on a side hustle from home, including financial rewards, improved work/life balance, and increased job satisfaction.

Financial Rewards: One of the most apparent benefits of stay-at-home side hustles is the potential for financial rewards.

Depending on the type of work you are doing, the amount of money you can make can vary greatly, but with the right skills and dedication, you can make a significant amount of extra money without leaving the house.

Improved Work/Life Balance: A side hustle can provide an outstanding balance between work and life.

You can work when it suits you while still having time to spend with your family, take care of other duties, or relax. You also don't have to worry about the dreaded morning commute or office politics.

Increased Job Satisfaction: A side hustle can provide great accomplishment and job satisfaction. Working on something you are passionate about can be incredibly rewarding and give you a sense of purpose. It can also help to boost your confidence and self-esteem.

Low Cost: You won't need to pay for expensive office space or other overhead costs when running a business from home. In the long run, this can help you save money.

Independence: You can be your boss and completely control your business. You can make decisions and take risks without worrying about someone else's approval.

Variety: You can choose from countless side hustle ideas to avoid boredom. You can also find something you're passionate about and make money doing it.

Growth Potential: A successful side hustle can provide an excellent opportunity for growth. You can use it as a stepping stone to launch a full-time business or career.

Tax Benefits: You can use tax deductions when running a business from home. These deductions can help you save money and provide extra income.

Networking Opportunities: You can build relationships with potential partners, customers, and mentors while running a side hustle. This can be beneficial for future business endeavors.

Passive Income: You can generate passive income by leveraging your time and skills to create products that can be sold repeatedly.

Personal Development: You can gain valuable skills and knowledge through your side hustle that can benefit you in other areas.

Satisfaction: A great sense of satisfaction comes from running a successful side hustle and seeing the fruits of your labor.

REAL-LIFE EXAMPLES OF SUCCESSFUL SIDE HUSTLERS

Many people have been successful with part-time jobs that they can do from home. Some people have even succeeded in transitioning their part-time jobs into full-time enterprises. For instance, a single mother, Sarah Titus, launched a blog as a stay-at-home side hustle when she first started raising her children.

Eventually, she transitioned the site into a full-time business that brings in more than six figures annually. Another good example is Nick Loper, who began working as a virtual assistant as a side hustle and is now the successful owner of an online firm that advises others on launching and developing their side businesses.

Paul Jarvis was a freelance web designer and author when he started his side hustle. He began by offering his services to a small group of clients, and his business multiplied. Paul eventually quit his day job and now works full-time as a freelance web designer. He has written several books on freelancing and has become a successful entrepreneur.

Dave Jacke was a software developer who had a passion for writing. He began blogging about his experiences, and soon his blog began to take off. He was able to monetize his blog and began earning an income. He eventually quit his day job to pursue blogging full-time and now makes a successful side income from his blog.

John Lee Dumas was a former military officer when he decided to take a chance on podcasting.

He started a weekly podcast, Entrepreneur On Fire, which quickly gained an audience of loyal listeners. John was able to monetize the show and eventually began making a full-time income from it. He now has multiple podcasts and makes a successful side income from them.

Natalie Sisson was a corporate lawyer when she decided to pursue her dream of becoming a digital nomad. She quit her job and began traveling the world while working remotely. She monetized her travels and made a successful side income from her blog and other digital projects.

These illustrations show that working on the side from home can be a lucrative method to make additional cash and perhaps pave the door for a new line of work. A wide variety of work can be done from home as a side hustle, and there is something for everyone to choose from. Some options include writing, teaching, and offering services such as house cleaning and pet sitting.

In conclusion, part-time jobs that can be done from home provide many benefits, such as flexibility, cheap initial investment requirements, and the opportunity to grow a part-time job into a full-time enterprise. A lucrative side business that can be done from home is now more accessible than ever before because of advances in technology and the proliferation of online platforms.

CHAPTER TWO

FINDING THE PERFECT STAY-AT-HOME SIDE HUSTLE

Finding the ideal stay-at-home side hustle can be difficult. With many alternatives available, deciding which is best for you might take time. Finding something that is both pleasant and profitable is the key. Here are some pointers to help you choose the perfect stay-at-home side hustle:

1. Evaluate Your Skills: Before you begin looking for side hustles, take some time to evaluate your abilities. What are your strong points? Do you have any interests or hobbies? What can you provide that others may not? Understanding your strengths can help you narrow down your alternatives when picking a side hustle.

2. Investigate Your Options: Once you've determined what you have to offer, begin looking into viable side hustles.

Search for opportunities that are a good fit for your skills and interests. Consider the potential for development and income, as well as the level of commitment necessary.

3. Choose a Niche: Once you've narrowed your selections, zero in on a niche. Seek options that allow you to specialize, such as pet sitting, virtual assistant work, or freelance writing. Beginning with specialization will help you quickly grow a customer base and enhance your talents.

4. Establish some attainable goals before you begin your side business quest. Please choose how much time you can dedicate to it and how much you want to generate. This will assist you in remaining focused and motivated.

5. Ultimately, action must be taken. Begin reaching out to potential clients, creating a blog, creating a website, or simply providing your services. The more accomplishments you achieve, the more successful you will become.

Discovering the proper stay-at-home side hustle can be difficult, but with little research, dedication, and hard work, you can find the perfect fit for you. Take risks and try new things; the experience can be quite rewarding.

DISCOVERING YOUR HOBBIES AND SKILLS

When starting a side hustle at home, it is critical to identify your hobbies and skills. Before you even contemplate what type of side hustle you want to pursue, think about what you enjoy doing, what you're excellent at, and what you're passionate about. When picking a side hustle, it will help you limit your alternatives and make the best decision.

To begin, write a list of all the activities you enjoy and are enthusiastic about. This can range from cooking and handicraft to writing and designing. Once you have this list, consider which activities you are good at and could improve on. Is there anything you've learned from hobbies or professions that you could use for a side hustle?

Next, assess your available resources. Do you own or have access to a computer? Are there any tools available to you that would be useful to you? Is there a special ability or information you possess that might be applied to a side hustle?

Next, consider the type of side hustle that would be most helpful to you. Do you want to make something that you can sell on the internet? Do you enjoy creating website content? Do you wish to use your abilities to assist others?

You'll determine the type of side hustle that suits you if you take the time to reflect on your hobbies and skills. This will ensure you can make the most of your time and resources while increasing your chances of success.

RESEARCHING POTENTIAL SIDE HUSTLES

Investigating prospective side hustles is an excellent way to boost your income while exploring new prospects.

Other potential side hustles to select from include freelance writing and online product sales. Before you commit to a side hustle, research to ensure it fits your abilities, hobbies, and lifestyle.

Begin by asking yourself what you're passionate about and what abilities and qualities you have to offer. Do you enjoy writing or designing? Are you well-organized and effective? Do you enjoy communicating with others? Understanding your abilities will assist you in narrowing down the kind of side hustles that may be a good fit for you.

Start investigating the many side hustles available once you've recognized your expertise. Numerous websites and forums are dedicated to side hustles, and reading reviews from others who have tried the side hustle you're interested in is a fantastic idea.

When exploring potential side hustles, keep the amount of time and work in mind.

Several side hustles, such as freelance writing or blogging, require significant time and effort to succeed. Before you go in, make sure you can make the necessary commitment.

Finally, remember to research a side venture's legal and tax ramifications. Depending on the nature of your side hustle, you may need to obtain permissions or licenses. Ensure you understand what is expected of you and take the appropriate steps to stay in compliance.

CONSIDERING EARNING POTENTIAL AND TIME COMMITMENT

When starting a side hustle at home, it is critical to consider both the money possibilities and the time commitment required to make it effective. The amount of money predicted to be produced from the side hustle is called income potential.

The quantity of time that will be committed to the side hustle is referred to as time commitment.

A few factors influence income potential. First, the sort of business must be determined. Will it be a service-based enterprise like freelance writing or web design? Will it be a product-based business, such as selling handmade products online? Understanding what type of business you have helps you assess your revenue potential.

Second, the level of work required to devote to the side hustle must be considered. Will this be a full-time job, or will it simply take a few hours daily? Understanding how much effort is required for the side hustle will assist in assessing the earning potential.

Lastly, a prospective consumer base must be identified. How many prospective clients are there, and how likely are they to buy the services or products? Understanding your possible consumer base will assist you in assessing your earning potential.

Many factors influence time commitment as well. First, the sort of business must be determined. Will the side hustle necessitate significant research and development time, or will it be primarily customer-facing? The type of business will determine the time commitment.

Second, the level of work required to devote to the side hustle must be considered. Will this take a long time, or can it be done in quick bursts? Understanding how much effort is required for the side hustle will assist in establishing the time commitment.

Lastly, the time required to market the side hustle must be considered. Will this take a long period, or can it be completed in quick bursts? Understanding how much time will be required to market the side hustle can assist you in evaluating your time commitment.

When determining the revenue potential and time commitment required to start a side hustle at home, consider the sort of business, the level of effort required, the possible customer base, and the amount of time required for marketing.

A well-planned side hustle can be a terrific way to earn extra money while working on something you enjoy that is personally satisfying.

CHAPTER THREE

TOP STAY-AT-HOME SIDE HUSTLES TO CONSIDER

WRITING FOR A LIVING

Freelance writing is a great supplement to income while working from home. Freelance writing may be a terrific side job for anyone, whether you're a stay-at-home mom, a student, or someone trying to supplement their income. Here are some helpful hints to get you started:

1. **Improve Your Writing Skills**: Because freelance writing is a competitive business, it is critical to have strong writing skills. Take the time to improve your writing skills and comprehend grammar and punctuation.

2. **Learn About Freelance Writing Markets:** Once you've honed your writing talents, it's time to look into freelance writing marketplaces. Search for websites and newspapers that pay for freelance pieces, or think about starting your blog to display your work.

3. **Discover Your Niche**: Pick topics that interest you and specialize in them. This will set you apart from other authors and make it easier for you to find work.

4. **Create a Portfolio**: Your portfolio is your calling card as a freelance writer. Put your best effort into it, and make sure it's up to date.

5. **Networking** is one of the most effective strategies for finding freelance writing opportunities. Contact coworkers, attend industry events, and join online organizations.

6. **Pitch**: Now that you've built your portfolio and network, it's time to start selling your services. Reach out to publications, websites, and other potential clients with a strong pitch, and you'll be well on your way to becoming a successful freelance writer.

Online job boards are a great place to start if you seek freelance writing opportunities. Numerous websites provide freelance writing jobs, including copywriting, blogging, technical, and creative writing.

Register with the job board and look for writing employment that matches your talents and interests. Make certain to carefully read the job descriptions and adapt your applications to the exact criteria.

Networking with other authors also helps you get freelance writing assignments.

Join social media writing groups, attend local writing events, or seek job posts on websites like ProBlogger, Freelance Writing Gigs, and Upwork.

Finally, construct a portfolio of writing samples that you may use to promote your services. Post your portfolio on social media, contact potential clients in your target industries, and inform them you are available for hire. You'll soon be able to find plenty of freelance writing jobs with a little effort.

ONLINE TUTORING

Online tutoring is a great stay-at-home side hustle for people who want to earn extra money while sharing their knowledge and skills with others. As the need for online education grows, online tutoring is becoming a more common option for giving educational services from a distance.

List your skills and areas of competence.
Establishing your abilities and expertise before beginning your online tutoring business is critical. Decide which subjects and levels you can teach. Consider getting relevant certificates or qualifications to boost your credibility and attract more clients.

Determine your target audience.
Choose your target audience depending on your abilities and expertise. Would you like to tutor youngsters or adults? Do you specialize in a topic, such as math or science?

Defining your target demographic will allow you to personalize your services and marketing activities to reach potential customers.

Establish a website and an online presence.
To get your online tutoring business off the ground, you must build a website and an online presence to promote your services and attract new clients. Your website should include information about your services, pricing, and client testimonials. You can also engage with potential clients and promote your services through social media platforms like Facebook, Twitter, and LinkedIn.

Choose an online tutoring platform.
Skype, Zoom, and Google Hangouts are just a few of the platforms accessible for online coaching. Choose a platform that is simple to use and includes capabilities that fit your requirements, such as video conferencing and screen sharing.

Establish your rates
Rates should be determined based on your experience, qualifications, and market demand. You can charge by the hour or session and offer package packages or discounts for large groups.

Make lesson plans and resources.
To deliver high-quality online tutoring services, you must develop lesson plans and resources that fit your clients' demands. Consider using internet resources such as Khan Academy or YouTube to enhance your teaching materials.

Market your products and services.

Use social media, internet forums, and word-of-mouth referrals to promote your online tutoring services.

Try paid advertising on social media channels to reach a larger audience.

Keep track of your schedule and workload.

To avoid burnout and stress, manage your schedule and workload as you would any other side hustle. Establish reasonable goals and manage your workload to ensure you have enough time to deliver high-quality teaching while keeping a healthy work-life balance.

VIRTUAL ASSISTANCE

Virtual assistance is a wonderful stay-at-home side job for anyone wishing to supplement their income. A virtual assistant (VA) is a self-employed individual who works from a distant location to provide administrative help to businesses and entrepreneurs. With the advancement of technology, an increasing number of organizations are hiring virtual assistants to aid them in managing administrative work, making virtual assistance an appealing and profitable side job.

Determining your abilities and services.

Defining your abilities and services before beginning your virtual assistant business is critical. Email management, social media management, customer support, data entry, and other services are provided by virtual assistants.

Determine which services you can provide to clients based on your abilities and experiences. You should also consider taking online classes or getting certified to boost your abilities and raise your earning potential.

Establishing your virtual assistant business
It's time to start your virtual assistant business now that you've selected your skills and services. You must build a website and social media presence to promote your services and attract new clients. Your website should highlight your abilities and services, and testimonials from prior clients can help you create credibility.

It would help to create a home office or workstation that promotes productivity and professionalism. Ascertain that you have the essential equipment to perform your services, such as a computer, internet connection, and phone.

Locating customers
Finding clients is one of the most important components of a successful virtual assistant business. You can find clients via networking on social media, attending virtual events, and directly approaching potential clients. Consider joining freelance markets like Upwork or Freelancer to obtain clients and jobs.

To sustain long-term clientele and a strong reputation, creating relationships with your clients and providing high-quality services is critical.

Rate setting and financial management
Establishing prices for your virtual assistant services can be difficult. While deciding your fees, consider your experience, talents, and market demand. You must also keep track of your expenses and revenue to manage your money effectively.

Finding a happy medium between your virtual assistant work and personal life
As with any side hustle, balancing your virtual assistant business and your personal life is critical. To minimize burnout and stress, set boundaries and focus on your workload. A support system, whether family, friends, or a virtual assistant community, is critical to help you manage your workload and achieve your objectives.

Launching a virtual assistant business is a great stay-at-home side hustle that provides flexibility and significant income potential. You may construct a profitable virtual assistant business from the comfort of your home by defining your skills and services, establishing your business, finding clients, managing your finances, and balancing your workload.

SOCIAL MEDIA ADMINISTRATION

Businesses require social media management to develop their online presence and acquire new clients.

Starting a social media management business might be a profitable side hustle if you have experience with social media platforms and are passionate about helping businesses thrive.

Choose your niche
Defining your specialization before beginning your social media management business is critical. Decide which industries or business types you want to work with, such as small enterprises, startups, or specific industries such as health and wellness or technology.

Improve your abilities
To be a successful social media manager, you must grasp numerous social media platforms, algorithms, and best practices. Consider attending classes or acquiring certificates to improve your skills and trustworthiness.

Develop a business plan
Create a business plan outlining your objectives, target audience, services, price, and marketing strategy. A business strategy can help you keep focused and guarantee that you are on the right track.

Establish your online presence
You must develop your online presence by creating a professional website and social media profiles in order to attract potential clients. Your website should include your services, pricing, and client testimonials. You can also use social media to demonstrate your knowledge and communicate with potential clients.

Plan your price approach

Develop a price strategy based on your experience, qualifications, and market demand. You can charge per project or offer monthly retainer packages with certain services included.

Create a portfolio

Create a portfolio of your work to demonstrate your expertise and attract future clients. Provide examples of social media campaigns you've handled and results and client testimonials.

Locate customers

You can use your network to find clients, use online marketplaces like Fiverr or Upwork, or reach out to potential clients directly. Networking with other professionals in your field can also aid in acquiring new clients.

Control your workload

Manage your workload like any other side hustle to avoid burnout and stress. Set realistic goals for yourself and prioritize your workload to ensure you can provide high-quality services while maintaining a healthy work-life balance.

DESIGNING GRAPHICS

Starting a graphic design business could be a great option if you have a passion for art and design and want to turn your talent into a profitable side hustle. These are some preliminary measures you can take:

Define your offerings.
It is critical to establish your services before beginning your graphic design firm.
Decide what kinds of design services you'll provide, such as logo design, web design, or print design. You can also focus on a specific industry, such as healthcare or technology.

Improve your abilities
To be a successful graphic designer, you must grasp design concepts, typography, color theory, and tools such as Adobe Photoshop and Illustrator. Consider attending classes or acquiring certificates to improve your skills and trustworthiness.

Make a business plan.
Create a business plan outlining your objectives, target audience, services, price, and marketing strategy. A business strategy can help you keep focused and guarantee that you are on the right track.

Create an internet presence for yourself.
To attract potential clients, you must develop your online presence by creating a professional website and social media profiles. Your website should include information about your services, pricing, and client testimonials. You can also use social media to demonstrate your knowledge and communicate with potential clients.

Decide on your pricing approach.
Develop a price strategy based on your experience, qualifications, and market demand. You can charge per project or by the hour.

Create a portfolio.
Create a portfolio of your design work to display and attract future clients. Provide examples of completed projects, results obtained, and client testimonials.

Locate customers
You can use your network to discover clients, use internet markets like Fiverr or Upwork, or reach out to potential clients directly. Networking with other professionals in your field can also aid in acquiring new clients.

Control your burden.
Manage your workload like any other side hustle to avoid burnout and stress. Establish reasonable objectives for yourself and prioritize your workload to guarantee you can provide high-quality services while keeping a healthy work-life balance.

Finally, beginning a graphic design firm can be a rewarding and lucrative side hustle. You can construct a profitable graphic design business from the comfort of your home by defining your services, improving your abilities, developing a business plan, building your internet presence, determining your pricing strategy, generating a portfolio, finding clients, and managing your workload.

BLOGGING

Establishing a blogging business as a side hustle from home might be a terrific way to supplement your income while pursuing your writing love. Here are some helpful hints to get you started:

Pick a niche: A niche is a specific topic or area of expertise on which your blog will focus. Select something about which you are enthusiastic and which has the potential to reach a huge audience. Personal finance, fashion, or health and well-being are all possibilities.

Pick a blogging platform: There are many blogging platforms, including WordPress, Blogger, and Squarespace. Select the one that best meets your demands and fits your budget. Consider aspects such as personalization, usability, and hosting costs.

Create your blog: Once you've decided on a platform, create your blog by picking a domain name and a theme and tweaking the design. Make sure your blog is visually appealing and simple to use.

Produce valuable material: Your content's quality will determine your blogging business's success. Make high-quality blog content that adds value to your readers' lives. Make your material more compelling by combining text, photos, and video.

Grow your audience: Use social media, email marketing, and other online marketing strategies to draw visitors to your site. Respond to comments and queries from your audience and solicit feedback.

Monetize your site: You may monetize your blog in a variety of ways, including advertising, affiliate marketing, sponsored content, and selling your own products or services. Pick the optimal monetization method for your specialty and audience.

Be consistent: When it comes to developing a successful blogging business, consistency is essential. Commit to regularly publishing high-quality material and engaging with your audience.

Starting a blogging business as a side hustle from home necessitates commitment, hard work, and perseverance. It can, however, be a profitable and enjoyable endeavor with the correct attitude and mindset.

PODCASTING

Podcasting has grown popular as a tool to communicate information and establish a following. It's a terrific method to start a side hustle and earn money from home. Here are some helpful hints to get you started:

Choose a topic: The first step in beginning a podcast is to select a topic about which you are enthusiastic. This range from cuisine to politics to technology.

The trick is to pick something about which you are knowledgeable and enthusiastic.

Research: Once you've decided on a topic, research to see what other podcasts are available on the same subject. This can help you figure out what works and what doesn't and discover a distinct approach that will set your podcast apart from the competitors.

Invest in equipment: You will need some basic equipment to start a podcast, such as a microphone, headphones, and a computer. You can spend a little money on these products, but it's crucial to invest in high-quality gear that produces decent sound.

Select a format: There are numerous podcast formats, including interviews, solo shows, and panel discussions. Consider which format would be best for your topic and audience.

Make a plan: Once you've decided on a topic, format, and equipment, it's time to plan your podcast. This should contain a recording and publication schedule and a strategy for advertising your podcast and growing an audience.

When you're ready to start recording, ensure you're in a peaceful place with no background noise. When you've recorded your episodes, you should carefully edit them to remove any errors or dead air.

Publish and promote: Once your episodes have been edited, upload them to a podcast hosting provider like Apple Podcasts, Spotify, or Stitcher. Marketing your podcast on social media and other means to grow your audience would be best.

Maintain consistency: Maintaining consistency is the key to creating a good podcast. This entails regularly publishing new episodes and connecting with your audience via social media and other ways.

Creating a podcast may be a rewarding and enjoyable side venture. With these suggestions, you can begin your podcasting journey from the comfort of your own home.

CHAPTER FOUR

STARTING YOUR STAY-AT-HOME SIDE HUSTLE

The First Step: **SETTING UP YOUR HOME OFFICE**

When beginning a side hustle that you can do from home, it is essential to set up a distinct workstation for yourself. To get your home office up and running efficiently, consider the following:

Locate a workspace that is exclusively yours.

In an ideal world, you would have a room in your house that was solely devoted to your side hustle. This could be a place in your main bedroom, a section of your living room, or even a spare room. Ensure that you have adequate illumination, a chair, and table or a workstation that are both comfortable for you and adequate lighting.

Remove distractions

When you work from home, it might be tempting to let yourself become sidetracked by things like domestic responsibilities, family members, or even pets. It would be best if you tried to get rid of as many distractions as possible by shutting the door, putting your phone on mute, and establishing clear boundaries with family members.

Invest in the appropriate pieces of equipment.

You may need to make some financial investments in various pieces of equipment to get started with your new side hustle. For instance, you'll need a computer and the appropriate software to establish your graphic design business. Whiteboards and other educational resources might be necessities for a new tutoring company, so keep that in mind.

CREATING A SCHEDULE AND STICKING TO IT

Keeping oneself motivated and engaged after beginning a work-from-home side business is one of the most difficult obstacles. The following is a list of suggestions for putting together a timetable and sticking to it:

Create a timetable.

Create a timetable for your side venture first and foremost. Choose when you want to begin and when you want to conclude it. This will help you keep on track and stay calm.

Divide it into manageable bits.

Once you've established a timetable, divide your side hustle into manageable parts. This can help you keep to your routine and avoid being overwhelmed.

Establish regular working hours.

Maintaining your concentration and output may be easier if you work daily hours. Determine a routine that functions well for you and adhere to it as much as possible.

Prioritize your tasks

Create a list of the things you need to accomplish each day, and then arrange the tasks in descending order of importance on the list. This will assist you in maintaining your concentration and ensuring that you are making progress toward the goals you have set for yourself.

Take breaks

It is essential to schedule pauses for yourself throughout the day so that you can refresh and revitalize. This might be as easy as walking around your neighborhood or participating in a brief yoga session.

Create a strategy.

Make sure you have a strategy for your side hustle.

This should include the tasks that must be completed and the timeframes for each assignment. This will help you keep organized and on track.

Make a timetable.

Create a schedule. Set aside time to focus on your side business.

Maintain your organization.

Ensure your workplace is well-organized and you have everything you need to complete the task. This will assist you in remaining focused and maximizing your efficiency.

Be bold and seek assistance.

Don't be afraid to seek assistance from family and friends. This will assist you in staying on track and motivated.

Reward yourself.

Finally, give yourself a prize for your efforts. This will help you stay motivated and continue your journey.

Following these tips will help you create and stick to a schedule when starting a side hustle at home. Remember that success requires hard effort and perseverance, so don't give up!

PROMOTING YOUR SERVICES

After preparing your home office and establishing a routine, it is time to begin promoting and selling your services. Here are some suggestions that can help you get the word out about your side hustle:

Establish an online website.

For any work-from-home gig to succeed, a website is absolutely necessary. It is an excellent method for displaying your company's services and delivering information about your company to prospective customers.

Utilize social media

When marketing your services, social media is a very effective strategy.

You should sign up for services like Facebook, Instagram, and Twitter, then utilize those accounts to market your company and interact with potential customers.

Engage with the people in your network.

It would be best always to appreciate the influence of your personal and professional connections. Try to get in touch with people you know personally, such as family members, acquaintances, and previous coworkers, to inform them about your side hustle and request their recommendations.

Experiment with Affiliate Marketing.

Affiliate marketing entails collaborating with other businesses or services to promote their products and services in exchange for a commission.

Take Use of Advertising Opportunities.

Paid advertising can be an excellent approach to spread the word swiftly. You can utilize Google AdWords, Facebook Ads, and other Internet advertising platforms to market your side hustle.

Advertise Locally.

Use local advertising mediums such as newspapers, radio, and billboards.

Provide Discounts or Coupons.

Providing discounts or coupons to new consumers is an excellent strategy to increase business.

Contact Influencers.

Reaching out to influencers can be a practical approach to promoting your business. Contact industry influencers and ask whether they would be ready to advertise your services.

Here are a few ideas for promoting your side business when you start. You may quickly spread the word and begin making money by utilizing these tactics.

MANAGING YOUR FINANCES

When you start a work-from-home side business, one of the most critical things you can do is ensure that your money is well managed. Here are some suggestions for maintaining organization in your financial affairs:

Create a Budget.

When you start your side business, develop a budget to assist you in understanding your financial restrictions and staying inside them. Assess the cost of supplies or services required to get your business up and to run.

Create a new bank account for your business.

If you want to keep better tabs on the money you make and spend from your side business, you should use a separate bank account.

Maintain a record of all of your expenditures.

Be sure to record your costs throughout the year, including the money you spend on supplies, equipment, and advertising.

Employ the services of a qualified individual.

If you are not confident in your ability to manage your money independently, consider hiring a professional accountant or bookkeeper to assist you in maintaining order and staying on top of your finances.

Having an Emergency Fund.

Emergency money is usually a good idea when establishing a side venture. This money might cover unforeseen needs or supplement your income if your side hustle generates less than you had intended.

Keep Personal and Company Costs Separate.

Keeping your personal and business spending distinct is critical. Get a separate company bank account and credit card to make it easier to track your expenditures.

Monitor Your Income and Expenses.

Tracking your income and expenses is critical for staying on top of your finances. Use an accounting system like QuickBooks or Wave to make this process easier.

Put Money Apart for Taxes.

When you begin a side hustle, you must set aside a portion of your earnings for taxes. Ensure you understand the tax regulations and any tax breaks you may be entitled to.

Invest in Your Side Hustle.

Investing in your side hustle might help you build your business and earn more money. Consider marketing, education, or new equipment investments.

Get Professional Assistance.

If you need help managing your funds, seek expert assistance. An accountant or financial advisor can help ensure you're on the right track.

Following these tips ensures your finances are in order when you start a side hustle. This will help you stay on top of your finances, avoid unexpected expenses, and make sure your business is booming.

CHAPTER FIVE

GROWING YOUR STAY-AT-HOME SIDE HUSTLE

If you want to transform your home-based side business into a full-time enterprise, you must concentrate on expanding it. Establishing a home-based side hustle is a fantastic way to generate additional money. Still, it would be best to concentrate on expansion to turn it into a full-time business. The following are some suggestions that can assist you in expanding your home-based side business:

EXPANDING YOUR SERVICES

Extending the range of services you provide is one of the first things you should do to see growth in your work-from-home side business. This could mean providing extra services inside your existing specialization or expanding out into an entirely new field. Here are some suggestions for broadening the scope of your existing offerings:

Recognize and capitalize on your best qualities.

Take some time to reflect on the skills you already possess and the areas in which you shine. Think about the several ways in which you might capitalize on those capabilities so that you can provide extra services to your customers.

Do research on the market you intend to compete in.

Do some market research to determine whether or not there is a need for the products or services you intend to expand into before you make any significant changes to your business. Look at what your rivals are up to, and see if you can spot any openings in the market.

Put your thoughts through the wringer.

Test your business expansion ideas on a limited number of existing or potential clients or consumers before committing significant time and resources to grow your company's offerings. This can assist you in determining how much interest there is in your new offerings and give you feedback on those offerings.

DEVELOPING YOUR BRAND

Growing your at-home side hustle requires establishing a solid brand name for your products or services. The following are some suggestions that can assist you in developing your brand:

Determine your brand values.

Consider what you want your brand to stand for and the core principles essential to you when making this decision. Keeping your brand's messaging and visual identity constant is one of the goals that this will assist you in achieving.

Create a distinct appearance for yourself.

Your company's logo, color palette, and any other visual elements you choose to represent your brand are all components of your company's visual identity. Create a visual identity that is consistent with your brand, embodies the values that your company stands for, and appeals to the audience you are trying to reach.

Develop a content strategy.

Building your brand and bringing in new customers are two goals that may be accomplished by developing a content strategy. Blogging, posting on social media, and creating other material that highlights your skill and personality are examples of what could fall under this category.

MAKING THE MOST OF YOUR POSSIBLE EARNINGS

To transform your part-time business from home into a full-time enterprise, you will need to concentrate on increasing the amount of money you can make from it. Here are some tips to help you get there:

Increase the cost of your goods and services.

Consider increasing your rates if you still need to get paid what you're worth. Because of this, you will be able to increase the amount of money you earn from the task that you are doing.

Provide packages or bundles.

Increasing your income and the value you bring to your customers by selling bundled or packaged goods can be a very effective approach to accomplish both goals. This could consist of a predetermined number of sessions or a combination of other types of services.

Develop sources of income that do not require active effort.

The generation of passive income streams enables one to continue earning money even when they are not actively engaged in earning that money. Creating an online course, penning an electronic book, or selling digital products fall under this category.

HIRING HELP AND SCALING UP

When the demand for your work-from-home side hustle increases, you may need additional assistance.

Here are some pointers to consider while expanding your business and employing new employees:

Determine what you need.

Consider which activities now use the majority of your time and whether or not you could benefit from having another person assist you with those activities. Work in administration, marketing, or assisting customers could fall into this category.

Organize and implement the necessary procedures and systems.

Set up procedures and processes for onboarding new customers, billing, and managing projects before scaling up your firm. This will guarantee that everything continues to function smoothly as you add more customers.

Efficiently distribute responsibility.

Your ability to successfully scale up your firm directly correlates to your ability to delegate tasks.

It would be best if you made sure that the employees you hire have the appropriate abilities and expertise, and you also need to make sure that you offer them clear instructions and expectations for their work.

Define Your Needs.

When you begin the process of recruiting help for your business, you must first clearly understand what jobs you require someone else to perform for it to flourish. This will assist you in narrowing down the type of assistance you require and the abilities required.

Establish Your Budget.

After you have defined your needs, you must establish your budget. This will allow you to filter down your list of possible hires and streamline the hiring process.

Create a Job Description.

When you begin the hiring process, creating a detailed job description is critical. Job duties, credentials, experience, and other pertinent information should be included.

Publish the Job

Once you've written a job description, you can start posting it online. Job boards, social media, and other recruitment tools can accomplish this.

Screen Candidates

After receiving job applications, screening the individuals to find the best fit for the job is critical. This should entail conducting interviews and checking references.

Hire.

Once you've found the best applicant for the job, it's time to make the hire. This includes drafting a contract, deciding payment methods, and outlining expectations.

Onboard and Train.

Once you've hired the necessary staff, onboarding and training them is critical. This ensures that they understand the tasks that need to be completed and how to do them.

Following these steps, you can easily hire help and scale up your side hustle business working from home. This will help you to increase your income and grow your business.

CHAPTER SIX

BALANCING YOUR STAY-AT-HOME SIDE HUSTLE WITH YOUR OTHER RESPONSIBILITIES

Starting a side business when caring for your children as a stay-at-home parent can be challenging. While also working on expanding your company, you might have to juggle several obligations, such as taking care of your children and completing domestic chores. Nevertheless, suppose you properly manage your time, establish clear boundaries, delegate tasks, and take steps to prevent burnout. In that case, you can attain a healthy balance in your life and succeed in your personal and professional endeavors.

STRATEGIES FOR EFFECTIVE TIME MANAGEMENT

Any individual who is responsible for many different things must understand the importance of efficient time management.

To be successful as a parent who stays at home while also running a side business, you need to learn how to organize your time and direct your attention to the pursuits that offer the most return. The following advice on how to better manage your time will assist you in striking a healthy balance between all of your obligations:

Make a plan: Plan out your day and divide it into segments, giving each one of your activities a certain amount of time. For instance, set out specific periods for your side job, domestic tasks, and childcare responsibilities throughout the day.

Concentrate on high-priority activities: At the beginning of each day, list the most important activities for you to finish, and then devote your full attention to completing those activities.

Eliminate Distractions: Stay away from things like social media and television if they can distract your attention from your task. Instead, it would help to focus on the most important things.

Utilize Technology: Make use of technology by utilizing productivity apps or software that can assist you in organizing your calendar, tracking your progress, and managing your time in the most effective manner possible.

Have Specific Goals: Before you begin your side hustle, know precisely what you want to achieve.

Please make a list of objectives and prioritize them in order of significance. This will assist you in remaining focused and organized.

Make a Schedule: To correctly manage your time while establishing a side hustle, schedule outlining when to work on specific activities. Make time for breaks and any unexpected duties that may arise.

Establish Boundaries: While beginning a side hustle, it is critical to establish boundaries not to overwork yourself and ignore other aspects of your life. Make time for yourself, your family, and other responsibilities.

Take Regular Breaks: When working on your side hustle, taking regular rests is critical. Taking pauses will help you maintain your motivation and stay focused when accomplishing activities.

Outsource Tasks: If you're swamped with tasks, consider outsourcing some to help you manage your time more effectively. Hiring a virtual assistant or a task-specific freelancer could be an option.

Monitor Your Time: Tracking your time can help you keep up with your tasks. Time-tracking software can help you track your time on each work and uncover areas where you might be more effective.

Delegate Tasks: Consider delegating part of the tasks to team members. This will free up your time and enable you to concentrate on more vital activities.

Use Automation: Automation can help you save time and simplify chores. Look for ways to automate tedious processes so that you may devote more time to more important responsibilities.

Prioritize Tasks: Prioritizing work based on importance is critical when launching a side hustle. Make a point of concentrating on the jobs that will have an enormous impact on your company.

ESTABLISHING BOUNDARIES

It is crucial to establish boundaries if you are a parent who stays at home while also running a side business. This will ensure you have the time and energy to fulfill your commitments. The following are some helpful hints about the establishment of boundaries:

Determine work hours: Inform your family of the hours you will be working on your side hustle and set clear goals for how much time you will spend working. Because of this, you can keep your job uninterrupted and free from distractions when you are scheduled to be there.

Please speak with your family: Tell your loved ones about your plans for the future, and make sure they understand the significance of your part-time job or other sources of income. They will have a better understanding of the need you have for boundaries as a result of this.

Get the skill of saying "no" and resist the temptation to take on new tasks that could cut into your time spent with your family or at work.

Create a Schedule: Making a plan for when you will and will not work on your side hustle can help you stay on track and avoid burnout. Provide realistic time frames for when you will be available and when you will be taking a break when planning your schedule. For example, you may work from 9 a.m. to 1 p.m. on Mondays and Wednesdays and from 9 a.m. to 3 p.m. on Fridays.

Maintain Organization: Maintaining organization is essential when handling your side hustle and personal life. Make a file system for your paperwork, a calendar to help you plan your days and weeks, and set reminders to help you remain on track.

Make Time for Yourself: A side hustle can be rewarding and draining. Set aside some time for yourself to relax and recharge. Making time for oneself is essential, whether going for a stroll, reading a book, or watching a movie.

Designate a Workspace: Designating a workstation will help you stay focused and organized. Locate a comfy and distraction-free location in your house.

If at all feasible, keep this office distinct from your home space. This will allow you to better distinguish between business and personal life.

Take Breaks: Working on a side hustle can be exhausting, so take rests throughout the day. Regular breaks will help you stay energized and motivated.

Have Fun: Remember to have fun while working on your side hustle. Working on something you adore may be gratifying and pleasurable, so make the most of the experience.

DELEGATING HOUSEHOLD CHORES

You can save time and energy by delegating domestic chores, allowing you to focus on your side business and other commitments. Here are some delegating tips:

Make a list of errands to run around the house and give each family member one or more of those jobs, considering their abilities and the amount of time they can devote to the endeavor.

Try contracting out some of your domestic responsibilities, such as the cleaning or the laundry, to a third party.

Develop a pattern: Establishing a pattern for daily activities, such as completing duties around the house, will help guarantee that these responsibilities are met continuously.

Create a schedule: Just like anything else, having a schedule for household duties is critical. This will ensure the family understands what is expected of them and when. It can also be beneficial to assign specific jobs to each employee and have a system to track progress.

Be adaptable: Working from home might make sticking to a regular schedule challenging. Be adaptable and change the schedule as needed. It's OK to rearrange things or give folks more time if required.

Make it enjoyable: Turn chores into a pleasant family activity. Turn monotonous work into a game or competition. This can motivate everyone and make the work more fun.

Make use of technology: Make use of technology to help manage domestic duties. Numerous apps and websites may assist you in tracking and assigning chores and setting reminders. This can help you keep organized.

Recognize and reward hard work: Everyone enjoys being recognized for their efforts. Reward employees that complete their tasks on time or go above and beyond. This will motivate everyone to continue their reasonable efforts.

By following these recommendations, you can ensure that everyone in the family is helping out around the house while still managing your work. You can find a strategy that works for everyone with patience and planning.

HOW TO PROTECT YOURSELF FROM BURNOUT

When you have a lot of different obligations to take care of at once, it's easy to become overwhelmed and exhausted. The following are some suggestions that should assist you in preventing from becoming burned out:

Take breaks: It is important to take breaks at regular intervals throughout the day to prevent exhaustion and maintain your energy levels.

Take care of yourself by obtaining adequate rest, eating correctly, and exercising consistently. This is an important aspect of self-care.

Locate a source of support by either becoming a group member for stay-at-home parents who are also engaged in side hustles or locating a mentor who can provide you with support and direction.

In conclusion, to maintain a healthy balance between your primary obligations and work-from-home side hustle, you must practice effective time management, establish clear boundaries, delegate tasks, and avoid burnout. You may succeed in both your personal and professional lives if you implement these strategies. You will be able to find a happy medium between the two.

CONCLUSION

Profitable Stay-At-Home Side Hustles is an in-depth guide for anyone wishing to earn extra money from the comfort of their own home. The book offers many practical and tried-and-true tactics for starting and growing a successful side hustle, including helpful hints on selecting profitable niches, marketing your services, and efficiently managing your time. This guide includes practical guidance and specific methods to help you achieve your financial objectives, whether you want to supplement your current income, pay off debt, or save for a rainy day. Everyone can turn their skills and passions into a profitable side business with the appropriate approach and persistence. This book is a must-read for everyone looking to gain financial control and create a better future for themselves and their loved ones.

Starting a stay-at-home side hustle might be a terrific way to supplement your income and improve your financial security.

Research, preparation, and dedication can create a profitable side business. The possibilities are limitless, from selling crafts online to offering virtual assistant services.

Furthermore, stay-at-home side hustles can provide the opportunity for a more flexible lifestyle. Several side hustles provide a more flexible schedule, allowing you to balance your other obligations while earning extra money.

By following the methods indicated in this book and conducting the necessary research, you may develop a successful, profitable side hustle that will provide you with the financial stability you require. You can transform your side hustle into a profitable business with hard effort and determination.

Overall, it would be best to do something other than limit your accomplishments with a side hustle from home. By devoting time to planning and research, you may build a successful and profitable business to achieve your aspirations.

You can attain success and realize your ambitions with the correct advice, determination, and a little hard effort.

Good luck on your journey toward financial freedom!

If you enjoyed this book, I will really appreciate a five star rating.

www.ingramcontent.com/pod-product-compliance
Lightning Source LLC
Chambersburg PA
CBHW070318240526
45467CB00046B/1653